PRINCEWILL LAGANG

Steve Ballmer: The Energetic Visionary

First published by PRINCEWILL LAGANG 2023

Copyright © 2023 by Princewill Lagang

All rights reserved. No part of this publication may be reproduced, stored or transmitted in any form or by any means, electronic, mechanical, photocopying, recording, scanning, or otherwise without written permission from the publisher. It is illegal to copy this book, post it to a website, or distribute it by any other means without permission.

Princewill Lagang asserts the moral right to be identified as the author of this work.

First edition

This book was professionally typeset on Reedsy.
Find out more at reedsy.com

Contents

1. Introduction — 1
2. Steve Ballmer: The Energetic Visionary — 2
3. Navigating Turbulence: Challenges and Triumphs — 4
4. The Windows of Opportunity: Ballmer's Vision for a New Era — 6
5. Pivot Points: Adapting to Change in the Mobile and Cloud Era — 8
6. Dynamics of Departure: Steve Ballmer's Exit from Microsoft — 10
7. Legacy Unveiled: Steve Ballmer's Impact on Microsoft's... — 12
8. Navigating the Clouds: Microsoft's Renaissance Under Satya... — 14
9. Embracing Diversity and Inclusion: Microsoft's Cultural... — 16
10. Charting the Future: Microsoft in the AI and Quantum... — 18
11. Microsoft's Global Impact: Technology for Social Good — 20
12. The Evolving Landscape: Microsoft in the Era of Intelligent... — 22
13. Cybersecurity Imperatives: Safeguarding the Digital Frontier — 24
14. Summary — 27

1

Introduction

Welcome to "Microsoft's Odyssey: Leadership, Innovation, and Impact in the 21st Century." In this exploration of one of the tech industry's titans, we embark on a journey spanning the energetic vision of Steve Ballmer to the transformative era under Satya Nadella's leadership. Microsoft, a global technology powerhouse, has not only weathered industry storms but also shaped the digital landscape. This book delves into key moments, strategic pivots, and the company's commitment to innovation, diversity, and societal impact. Join us as we navigate the highs, lows, and evolution of Microsoft in the ever-changing realm of 21st-century technology.

2

Steve Ballmer: The Energetic Visionary

The morning sun cast a warm glow over the bustling streets of Detroit as Steve Ballmer, the man with boundless energy and an unwavering vision, stepped onto the stage at the Cobo Center. The year was 2000, and the world was on the cusp of a technological revolution. As the CEO of Microsoft, Ballmer was about to deliver a keynote address that would set the tone for the next era of computing.

The chapter opens with a vivid scene, painting the backdrop of a significant moment in Steve Ballmer's career. The choice of Detroit, a city known for its resilience and innovation, sets the stage for the transformative journey that Ballmer is about to embark upon.

The narrative then delves into Steve Ballmer's early life, exploring the formative experiences that shaped the man behind the energetic visionary. From his childhood in Detroit to his academic pursuits at Harvard, we gain insights into the factors that contributed to Ballmer's development as a leader. The chapter highlights key moments, such as his meeting with Bill Gates at Harvard, which set the course for his future endeavors.

STEVE BALLMER: THE ENERGETIC VISIONARY

As Ballmer takes the stage in 2000, the chapter transitions to an exploration of Microsoft's role in the tech landscape. The reader is introduced to the state of the industry at that time, with the dot-com boom in full swing. Microsoft, under Ballmer's leadership, faced both unprecedented opportunities and challenges. The chapter delves into the dynamics of the technology landscape, providing a comprehensive understanding of the context in which Ballmer was operating.

The narrative skillfully weaves in anecdotes and quotes from Ballmer's contemporaries, providing a multi-faceted perspective on the man and his vision. Colleagues, friends, and industry experts share their impressions, adding depth to the portrayal of Ballmer as a dynamic and charismatic leader.

The energetic atmosphere of the keynote address is palpable as Ballmer articulates his vision for the future. The chapter explores the key points of his speech, ranging from the importance of software in a connected world to his bold predictions about the role of technology in reshaping industries.

To conclude the chapter, the narrative hints at the challenges and controversies that would later define Ballmer's tenure at Microsoft. The reader is left with a sense of anticipation, eager to uncover the intricacies of Ballmer's journey as the narrative unfolds in subsequent chapters.

3

Navigating Turbulence: Challenges and Triumphs

As the echoes of Steve Ballmer's passionate keynote address at the Cobo Center lingered, the tech industry entered a period of unprecedented turbulence. The year was 2000, and Microsoft, under Ballmer's leadership, faced challenges that would test the mettle of even the most seasoned visionaries.

The chapter begins by delving into the aftermath of the keynote, exploring how Ballmer's vision resonated with the tech community and investors. It then transitions seamlessly into the evolving landscape of the early 2000s, marked by the bursting of the dot-com bubble, heightened competition, and regulatory scrutiny. The narrative examines how these external forces shaped Microsoft's strategies and decision-making during this critical period.

The chapter explores Ballmer's leadership style and his approach to steering Microsoft through rough waters. Drawing on interviews with colleagues and industry experts, the narrative provides a nuanced understanding of how Ballmer's energy and determination influenced the company's culture and response to challenges.

A central focus of this chapter is Microsoft's legal battles and regulatory challenges. The antitrust case against Microsoft, led by the Department of Justice, unfolds as a pivotal moment in the company's history. The narrative details the courtroom drama, the public perception, and the impact on Microsoft's business strategies. Ballmer's role in navigating this legal quagmire is examined, shedding light on his resilience in the face of adversity.

The chapter doesn't shy away from exploring internal dynamics within Microsoft during this period. The reader gains insight into how Ballmer managed the company's diverse teams, fostering innovation and addressing internal challenges. Personal anecdotes and interviews with key figures within the company contribute to a comprehensive portrayal of the corporate environment during these tumultuous years.

Amidst the challenges, the chapter highlights triumphs and milestones. Microsoft's forays into new product launches, strategic partnerships, and innovations in software development are explored. The narrative showcases instances where Ballmer's vision translated into tangible successes, illustrating his ability to pivot and adapt in a rapidly changing industry.

As the chapter concludes, the reader is left with a sense of anticipation, eager to witness how Steve Ballmer's leadership will continue to shape Microsoft's trajectory. The narrative sets the stage for the subsequent chapters, which will delve into the evolving landscape of technology and Ballmer's enduring impact on the industry.

4

The Windows of Opportunity: Ballmer's Vision for a New Era

Entering the early 21st century, Steve Ballmer faced a pivotal moment in his tenure at Microsoft. The tech industry was evolving rapidly, and the visionary leader was determined to guide the company through a series of transformative initiatives. This chapter explores Ballmer's strategic vision, honing in on the development and launch of key products that would define Microsoft's role in the digital era.

The chapter opens with the atmosphere within Microsoft as Ballmer, fueled by his characteristic energy, spearheads a renewed focus on software and operating systems. The reader is introduced to the challenges and opportunities presented by the changing landscape, with the rise of mobile computing, the advent of smartphones, and the increasing importance of cloud services.

A significant portion of the chapter is dedicated to the development and release of Windows XP, a flagship operating system that aimed to bridge the gap between personal and professional computing. The narrative delves into the technical innovations, design philosophies, and market strategies behind Windows XP, offering a behind-the-scenes look at Microsoft's efforts to maintain its dominance in the operating system space.

As the story unfolds, the chapter transitions to Microsoft's exploration of the mobile market. Ballmer's strategic decisions, including the launch of Windows Mobile and later the Windows Phone, are scrutinized. The narrative explores the challenges Microsoft faced in gaining traction in the mobile space, including competition from industry giants like Apple and Google.

The reader is taken through the highs and lows of Ballmer's ambitious initiatives, including the acquisition of Nokia's mobile division. Personal interviews with key players in Microsoft during this period provide valuable insights into the decision-making processes, successes, and setbacks.

In parallel, the chapter explores Microsoft's entry into the realm of cloud computing. Ballmer's recognition of the transformative power of the cloud is highlighted, along with the strategic moves to position Microsoft as a major player in the cloud services market. The development of Azure, Microsoft's cloud platform, becomes a focal point, showcasing the company's ability to adapt to emerging trends.

As the chapter concludes, the reader is left with a sense of the dynamic and evolving nature of the tech industry and Ballmer's relentless pursuit of innovation. The narrative sets the stage for the subsequent chapters, where the exploration of Microsoft's journey under Ballmer's leadership will continue to unfold.

5

Pivot Points: Adapting to Change in the Mobile and Cloud Era

The turn of the decade marked a critical juncture for Steve Ballmer and Microsoft. The technology landscape continued to shift, with the proliferation of smartphones, the ascent of mobile apps, and the rapid growth of cloud computing. This chapter delves into how Ballmer navigated these pivotal moments, steering Microsoft through challenges while leveraging new opportunities.

The narrative begins with the rise of smartphones and the transformative impact of the iPhone and Android devices. Ballmer's response to the changing dynamics of the mobile industry takes center stage. The chapter explores Microsoft's endeavors in mobile, including the evolution of the Windows Phone platform, strategic partnerships, and the challenges faced in gaining market share.

Amidst the exploration of mobile endeavors, the narrative weaves in the dynamics of Microsoft's competition with Apple and Google. Interviews with industry insiders shed light on the strategies employed by Ballmer to

PIVOT POINTS: ADAPTING TO CHANGE IN THE MOBILE AND CLOUD ERA

position Microsoft in the highly competitive mobile ecosystem. The chapter also reflects on the significance of the "app economy" and how it influenced Microsoft's approach to software development.

A significant portion of the chapter is dedicated to the bold move by Microsoft to enter the hardware market with the Surface tablet. The narrative unfolds the decision-making process behind this strategic pivot, shedding light on Ballmer's vision for creating a seamless integration of hardware and software. Interviews with key figures within Microsoft provide a firsthand account of the challenges and triumphs associated with this venture.

As the narrative progresses, the focus shifts to the growing prominence of cloud computing. Ballmer's recognition of the strategic importance of cloud services for the future of technology is explored. The chapter delves into the development and expansion of Microsoft Azure, detailing the challenges faced and the milestones achieved as the company sought to establish itself as a leader in cloud computing.

Simultaneously, the reader gains insight into Ballmer's leadership style during this transformative period. Personal anecdotes and interviews with colleagues provide a nuanced understanding of how Ballmer motivated teams, made strategic decisions, and addressed the complexities of managing a tech giant in an era of rapid change.

The chapter concludes with a reflection on the evolving perception of Microsoft under Ballmer's leadership. The reader is left with a sense of anticipation, eager to uncover how Microsoft's journey continues to unfold in the face of ongoing technological advancements and industry shifts.

6

Dynamics of Departure: Steve Ballmer's Exit from Microsoft

As the second decade of the 21st century progressed, the tech industry witnessed a series of seismic shifts. Steve Ballmer, the energetic visionary at the helm of Microsoft, found himself grappling with challenges that would ultimately shape the final chapters of his tenure. This chapter explores the events leading up to Steve Ballmer's departure from Microsoft, examining the internal and external factors that played a role in this significant transition.

The narrative opens with the evolving landscape of the technology industry, marked by the continued rise of competitors, changes in consumer preferences, and the growing influence of new players in the market. Against this backdrop, Ballmer faced increasing scrutiny from investors and industry analysts questioning Microsoft's ability to innovate and remain at the forefront of technological advancements.

The chapter delves into the reception and impact of major product launches, including Windows 8 and the Microsoft Surface, shedding light on how these initiatives were perceived both within the company and by the broader tech community. Interviews with key stakeholders provide insights into the decision-making processes and the challenges faced in bringing these products to market.

Simultaneously, the narrative explores the internal dynamics at Microsoft, including shifts in leadership roles, changes in organizational structure, and the evolving corporate culture. The chapter examines how these internal factors influenced decision-making at the executive level and contributed to the mounting pressure on Ballmer to deliver transformative results.

One of the focal points of the chapter is the "One Microsoft" reorganization initiative, a strategic effort to streamline operations and foster greater collaboration within the company. The narrative delves into the objectives, challenges, and outcomes of this initiative, offering a comprehensive understanding of its impact on Microsoft's trajectory.

As the story unfolds, the chapter addresses the challenges posed by activist investors and their impact on Ballmer's leadership. The narrative explores the board's response to shareholder concerns and the intensifying calls for a change in leadership. Interviews with board members, insiders, and industry analysts provide diverse perspectives on the events leading up to Ballmer's decision to step down as CEO.

The chapter concludes with the announcement of Ballmer's departure and reflects on his legacy at Microsoft. The reader is left with a sense of the complex interplay of internal and external factors that contributed to this significant moment in the company's history. Subsequent chapters will continue to unravel the post-Ballmer era at Microsoft and explore the lasting impact of his leadership on the tech giant.

7

Legacy Unveiled: Steve Ballmer's Impact on Microsoft's Evolution

The departure of Steve Ballmer marked a turning point in Microsoft's history. This chapter delves into the aftermath of his exit, exploring the immediate effects and the lasting impact of Ballmer's leadership on the company's evolution.

The narrative opens with the announcement of Satya Nadella as Ballmer's successor. The chapter explores the initial reactions from both within and outside Microsoft, shedding light on the expectations and challenges faced by Nadella as he stepped into the role of CEO. Interviews with key figures in the transition provide insights into the decision-making process and the strategic vision that Nadella brought to the table.

A significant portion of the chapter is dedicated to an analysis of Ballmer's legacy. The narrative evaluates the successes and challenges of his tenure, examining the key initiatives and decisions that shaped Microsoft's trajectory during his leadership. Interviews with industry analysts, Microsoft employees, and contemporaries provide diverse perspectives on the impact of Ballmer's energetic and visionary approach.

The chapter also reflects on the ongoing transformation within Microsoft initiated by Ballmer, particularly the "One Microsoft" reorganization. The reader gains insights into how this strategic shift influenced the company's culture, innovation, and collaboration, laying the groundwork for the changes that would continue under Nadella's leadership.

As the narrative progresses, the chapter explores Microsoft's performance in the post-Ballmer era, analyzing financial results, market positioning, and the reception of new products and services. Interviews with key stakeholders offer perspectives on how the company adapted to emerging technologies and market trends, showcasing the resilience and adaptability fostered during Ballmer's tenure.

The narrative doesn't shy away from addressing the criticisms and challenges faced by Microsoft during this period. The chapter examines how the company responded to evolving consumer preferences, increasing competition, and the need to stay relevant in a rapidly changing tech landscape. The reader gains a comprehensive understanding of the strategic decisions made under Nadella's leadership and their implications for Microsoft's future.

In conclusion, the chapter reflects on the enduring impact of Steve Ballmer's legacy on Microsoft. The reader is left with a nuanced understanding of how Ballmer's energetic and visionary leadership laid the foundation for the company's ongoing evolution. Subsequent chapters will explore Microsoft's journey further into the 21st century, examining the company's response to new challenges and opportunities.

8

Navigating the Clouds: Microsoft's Renaissance Under Satya Nadella

With Satya Nadella at the helm, Microsoft entered a new era defined by a relentless focus on the cloud, innovation, and a growth mindset. This chapter explores the transformative journey of Microsoft under Nadella's leadership, tracing the company's renaissance in the face of evolving industry trends.

The narrative opens with Nadella's vision for Microsoft, emphasizing a cloud-first, mobile-first strategy. The chapter examines the strategic shifts in product development, organizational culture, and market positioning initiated by Nadella. Interviews with key executives and insiders provide insights into the decision-making processes and the cultural transformation that defined this period.

A significant portion of the chapter is dedicated to the development and expansion of Microsoft Azure, the cloud computing platform. The narrative delves into the strategic decisions, technical innovations, and market dynamics that propelled Azure to the forefront of the cloud services industry. The reader gains a comprehensive understanding of how Nadella's emphasis on cloud computing played a pivotal role in Microsoft's resurgence.

The narrative also explores Microsoft's strategic acquisition of LinkedIn, shedding light on the motivations behind this significant move and its impact on Microsoft's ecosystem. Interviews with executives involved in the acquisition provide insights into the integration process and the synergies realized through this strategic partnership.

Simultaneously, the chapter traces the evolution of key Microsoft products, including Windows 10 and the Microsoft Surface line. The narrative examines how Nadella's leadership influenced the development and marketing strategies, emphasizing a more collaborative and customer-centric approach.

The reader is taken through Microsoft's foray into artificial intelligence (AI) and mixed reality, showcasing the company's commitment to staying at the forefront of technological innovation. The chapter delves into the development of products like HoloLens and the incorporation of AI into various Microsoft services, illustrating the company's efforts to shape the future of computing.

As the narrative progresses, the chapter reflects on Microsoft's financial performance, market positioning, and its reception in the industry. Interviews with industry analysts and stakeholders offer diverse perspectives on Microsoft's resurgence under Nadella's leadership.

The chapter concludes with a reflection on the broader implications of Microsoft's renaissance, not only for the company itself but for the tech industry as a whole. The reader is left with a sense of anticipation, eager to explore how Microsoft's journey will continue to unfold in the dynamic landscape of the 21st century.

9

Embracing Diversity and Inclusion: Microsoft's Cultural Transformation

In the midst of technological advancements and strategic shifts, Satya Nadella embarked on a mission to transform not just Microsoft's products and services but also its internal culture. This chapter explores Microsoft's journey towards becoming a more diverse, inclusive, and innovative workplace under Nadella's leadership.

The narrative opens with an examination of Nadella's early initiatives to foster cultural change within Microsoft. The chapter delves into his commitment to diversity and inclusion, emphasizing the importance of a workforce that reflects the global communities the company serves. Interviews with employees and diversity advocates provide personal insights into the cultural shifts underway.

A significant portion of the chapter is dedicated to the launch of the book "Hit Refresh" by Satya Nadella, where he articulates his vision for Microsoft's culture. The narrative explores how the book became a manifesto for the company's cultural transformation, emphasizing empathy, learning from failure, and a growth mindset. It reflects on how these principles permeated through the organization, influencing decision-making, collaboration, and innovation.

The chapter also examines the implementation of specific programs and initiatives aimed at promoting diversity and inclusion within Microsoft. From unconscious bias training to the expansion of employee resource groups, the narrative illustrates the multifaceted approach taken by the company to create an inclusive workplace. Interviews with employees who participated in these programs offer firsthand accounts of their impact.

Simultaneously, the chapter explores Microsoft's broader initiatives to address societal challenges related to diversity and technology. The narrative reflects on the company's commitment to closing the digital divide, promoting STEM education, and leveraging technology for social impact. The reader gains an understanding of how Microsoft, under Nadella's leadership, sought to be a responsible corporate citizen.

As the story unfolds, the chapter delves into the ongoing efforts to measure and assess the impact of cultural transformation at Microsoft. Metrics related to diversity, employee satisfaction, and innovation are explored, providing a comprehensive view of the outcomes of the company's initiatives.

The chapter concludes with a reflection on the broader implications of Microsoft's cultural transformation, not only for the company but for the tech industry as a whole. The reader is left with an understanding of how Nadella's leadership has not only reshaped Microsoft's internal culture but has also positioned the company as a beacon for positive change in the technology sector. Subsequent chapters will continue to explore Microsoft's journey and its impact on the evolving landscape of the 21st century.

10

Charting the Future: Microsoft in the AI and Quantum Computing Era

As the 21st century unfolded, Microsoft found itself at the forefront of transformative technologies, with Satya Nadella steering the company into uncharted territory. This chapter explores Microsoft's endeavors in the realms of artificial intelligence (AI) and quantum computing, showcasing the company's commitment to shaping the future of computing.

The narrative opens with an exploration of Microsoft's foray into AI, examining how Nadella's leadership positioned the company as a key player in the development and deployment of artificial intelligence technologies. The chapter delves into the integration of AI into various Microsoft products and services, illustrating how the company harnessed the power of machine learning to enhance user experiences and drive innovation.

A significant portion of the chapter is dedicated to Microsoft's strategic investments in research and development, particularly in the field of quantum computing. The narrative explores the company's ambitious Quantum Computing initiative, shedding light on the technical challenges, breakthroughs, and the potential impact of quantum computing on the future of technology. Interviews with key figures within Microsoft's Quantum Computing division provide insights into the intricacies of this groundbreaking endeavor.

Simultaneously, the chapter examines Microsoft's collaborations with research institutions, startups, and industry partners in the AI and quantum computing space. The narrative reflects on the importance of fostering a collaborative ecosystem to advance these cutting-edge technologies, showcasing how Microsoft positioned itself as a catalyst for industry-wide innovation.

As the story unfolds, the chapter explores the ethical considerations associated with AI and quantum computing. The narrative reflects on Microsoft's commitment to responsible and ethical development, highlighting initiatives related to privacy, transparency, and the ethical use of AI. The reader gains an understanding of how Nadella's leadership prioritized these considerations in the pursuit of technological advancements.

The chapter also delves into the market implications of Microsoft's endeavors in AI and quantum computing. The narrative reflects on how these technologies positioned the company in a competitive landscape, influencing partnerships, market positioning, and the broader technological ecosystem.

As the narrative progresses, the chapter concludes with a reflection on the broader implications of Microsoft's ventures into AI and quantum computing. The reader is left with a sense of anticipation, eager to explore how these technologies will shape the future of Microsoft and the tech industry at large in the coming years. Subsequent chapters will continue to unravel the unfolding story of Microsoft's role in the evolving technological landscape.

11

Microsoft's Global Impact: Technology for Social Good

Beyond the realms of business and innovation, Satya Nadella's Microsoft has sought to leverage technology for positive societal impact. This chapter delves into Microsoft's initiatives aimed at addressing global challenges, promoting accessibility, and utilizing technology for social good under Nadella's leadership.

The narrative opens with an exploration of Microsoft's commitment to addressing societal challenges through technology. The chapter examines initiatives such as AI for Earth and AI for Accessibility, showcasing how Microsoft harnessed the power of artificial intelligence to tackle environmental issues and enhance accessibility for people with disabilities. Interviews with key figures involved in these programs provide insights into the motivations and outcomes of these endeavors.

A significant portion of the chapter is dedicated to Microsoft's philanthropic efforts, including the creation of the Microsoft Philanthropies division. The narrative explores the company's commitment to providing technology access to underserved communities, promoting digital literacy, and addressing the global digital divide. The reader gains an understanding of how Microsoft positioned itself as a responsible corporate citizen with a focus on making a positive impact on a global scale.

Simultaneously, the chapter examines Microsoft's involvement in addressing pressing global challenges, including healthcare initiatives, disaster response efforts, and humanitarian projects. The narrative reflects on how the company collaborated with NGOs, governments, and international organizations to deploy technology in innovative ways to address complex societal issues.

The chapter also delves into Microsoft's commitment to sustainability, reflecting on initiatives to reduce the company's environmental impact and promote a more sustainable future. The reader gains insight into Microsoft's efforts to harness renewable energy, reduce carbon emissions, and contribute to the global fight against climate change.

As the story unfolds, the chapter explores the role of technology in education and skill development. The narrative reflects on Microsoft's initiatives to empower individuals with the skills needed for the jobs of the future, emphasizing the importance of lifelong learning and digital literacy.

The chapter concludes with a reflection on the broader implications of Microsoft's commitment to technology for social good. The reader is left with an understanding of how Nadella's leadership positioned Microsoft as a company with a purpose, leveraging technology to address some of the most pressing challenges facing the world. Subsequent chapters will continue to explore Microsoft's multifaceted impact on the global stage.

12

The Evolving Landscape: Microsoft in the Era of Intelligent Cloud and Edge

As the second decade of the 21st century unfolded, Microsoft found itself navigating an ever-evolving technological landscape. This chapter explores the company's strategic responses to emerging trends, with a focus on the era of the intelligent cloud and edge computing under Satya Nadella's leadership.

The narrative opens with an examination of the increasing importance of cloud computing and edge technologies. The chapter delves into how Microsoft positioned itself at the forefront of these trends, emphasizing the integration of intelligent cloud services with edge computing capabilities. Interviews with key executives and technologists provide insights into the decision-making processes and the technical innovations driving this transformation.

A significant portion of the chapter is dedicated to the expansion and evolution of Microsoft Azure, the company's cloud computing platform. The narrative explores the introduction of new services, the growth of data centers globally, and the strategic partnerships that further solidified Azure's position in the highly competitive cloud services market. The reader gains an understanding of how Nadella's focus on the intelligent cloud became a linchpin in Microsoft's broader strategy.

Simultaneously, the chapter delves into the concept of edge computing, highlighting Microsoft's initiatives to bring computing power closer to where data is generated. The narrative explores the development of Azure IoT Edge and other edge computing solutions, showcasing how Microsoft enabled organizations to harness the benefits of real-time processing and analysis.

The narrative also reflects on the role of artificial intelligence (AI) in this evolving landscape. The reader gains insights into how Microsoft infused AI capabilities into its cloud services, providing organizations with tools to extract valuable insights from vast amounts of data. The chapter explores real-world applications of AI in diverse industries, from healthcare to manufacturing, illustrating the transformative potential of intelligent cloud and edge solutions.

As the story unfolds, the chapter explores Microsoft's approach to hybrid cloud solutions, acknowledging the reality that many organizations operate in a hybrid IT environment. The narrative reflects on how Microsoft provided tools and services that seamlessly bridged on-premises data centers and cloud resources, offering flexibility and scalability to businesses worldwide.

The chapter concludes with a reflection on the broader implications of Microsoft's strategic focus on the intelligent cloud and edge. The reader is left with an understanding of how these technologies have become integral to Microsoft's vision for the future and the company's ongoing role in shaping the digital landscape. Subsequent chapters will continue to unravel Microsoft's journey as it navigates the complexities of the 21st-century technology ecosystem.

13

Cybersecurity Imperatives: Safeguarding the Digital Frontier

In an era defined by digital interconnectedness, the need for robust cybersecurity measures became paramount. This chapter explores Microsoft's role in addressing cybersecurity challenges and fostering a secure digital environment under the leadership of Satya Nadella.

The narrative opens with an examination of the evolving cybersecurity landscape, marked by increasingly sophisticated cyber threats, ransomware attacks, and state-sponsored cyber espionage. The chapter delves into how Nadella's Microsoft responded to these challenges, emphasizing a comprehensive and integrated approach to cybersecurity.

A significant portion of the chapter is dedicated to Microsoft's initiatives to strengthen the security of its products and services. The narrative explores the integration of advanced threat protection mechanisms into Windows, Office 365, and Azure, showcasing how the company sought to provide users with robust defenses against evolving cyber threats. Interviews with cybersecurity experts within Microsoft provide insights into the technical innovations driving these efforts.

Simultaneously, the chapter delves into Microsoft's commitment to fostering a safer internet for all users. The narrative explores initiatives such as the Digital Crimes Unit and the Cyber Threat Intelligence Program, illustrating how Microsoft collaborated with law enforcement agencies, industry partners, and cybersecurity researchers to combat cybercrime globally.

The narrative also reflects on Microsoft's efforts to empower organizations with tools and resources to enhance their own cybersecurity postures. The chapter explores the development and promotion of security best practices, the implementation of cybersecurity training programs, and the role of Microsoft's cybersecurity services in helping organizations detect and respond to threats effectively.

As the story unfolds, the chapter examines the role of artificial intelligence (AI) and machine learning in Microsoft's cybersecurity strategy. The narrative reflects on how these technologies were employed to analyze vast amounts of data, identify patterns indicative of cyber threats, and enable proactive threat detection and response.

The chapter also explores Microsoft's engagement with the broader cybersecurity community, including participation in industry collaborations, information-sharing initiatives, and the responsible disclosure of security vulnerabilities. The reader gains an understanding of how Microsoft's commitment to transparency and collaboration contributed to a collective defense against cyber threats.

The chapter concludes with a reflection on the ongoing challenges and future directions in cybersecurity. The reader is left with an appreciation of Microsoft's multifaceted approach to safeguarding the digital frontier and the company's role in shaping the cybersecurity landscape for a more secure digital future. Subsequent chapters will continue to explore Microsoft's journey as it navigates the complexities of the digital age.

14

Summary

In this comprehensive exploration of Microsoft's journey spanning several chapters, we trace the evolution of the technology giant under the leadership of Steve Ballmer and Satya Nadella. The narrative begins with Ballmer's energetic vision, detailing key moments in his leadership, from navigating the dot-com bubble to facing antitrust challenges. The subsequent chapters delve into the strategic shifts under Nadella, examining Microsoft's forays into mobile, cloud computing, and the cultural transformation fostering diversity and inclusion.

The narrative then unfolds the chapters on Microsoft's response to emerging technologies like AI and quantum computing, showcasing the company's commitment to shaping the future of computing. Additionally, Microsoft's global impact and philanthropic initiatives, focusing on societal challenges and sustainability, are explored.

The later chapters shed light on Microsoft's strategic positioning in the era of the intelligent cloud and edge computing, emphasizing the integration of AI into cloud services. Furthermore, the narrative highlights Microsoft's commitment to cybersecurity, detailing initiatives to strengthen security measures, collaborate with the cybersecurity community, and use AI for threat detection.

Collectively, these chapters provide a nuanced portrait of Microsoft's journey, illustrating how the company adapted to industry shifts, embraced innovation, and addressed societal challenges. From energetic visions to cultural transformations and technological advancements, Microsoft's story unfolds as a dynamic narrative of leadership, resilience, and a commitment to positive global impact in the ever-evolving landscape of the 21st century.